THE BEST
DOGS
EVER

POMERANIANS ARE THE BEST!

Elaine Landau

LERNER PUBLICATIONS COMPANY · MINNEAPOLIS

For Ellen Ruffin

Lerner Publications Company
A division of Lerner Publishing Group, Inc.
241 First Avenue North
Minneapolis, MN 55401 U.S.A.

Website address: www.lernerbooks.com

Library of Congress Cataloging-in-Publication Data

Landau, Elaine.
  Pomeranians are the best! / by Elaine Landau.
      p.   cm. — (The best dogs ever)
  Includes index.
  ISBN 978-0-7613-5057-6 (lib. bdg. : alk. paper)
  1. Pomeranian dog—Juvenile literature. I. Title.
 SF429.P8L36 2011
 636.76—dc22   2009016422

Manufactured in the United States of America
1 — BP — 7/15/10

TABLE OF CONTENTS

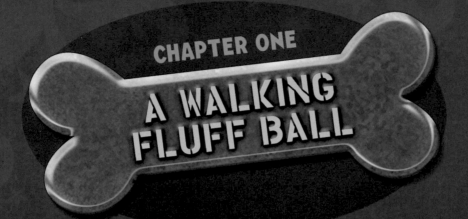

CHAPTER ONE
A WALKING FLUFF BALL

Could you fall for a tiny dog with a powder-puff coat? Some say this dog looks like a little lion. Others say it looks like a miniature fox. Still others have called it a fluff ball on four feet.

Can you guess the dog I'm talking about? This pom-pom of a pooch is a **Pomeranian.** These canine cuties are called Poms for short.

A Teeny Tiny Pal

Poms are solid, sturdy dogs. They're also small enough to fit in a tote bag! These dogs weigh from 3 to 7 pounds (1 to 3 kilograms). You may have had teddy bears bigger than a Pom.

Pretty Pooches

Poms are bright eyed and beautiful. Its fur is this dog's crowning glory. Poms have long, thick, silky, double coats.

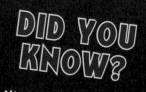

DID YOU KNOW?

Dogs with double coats have two layers of fur. One layer is short and lies close to the dog's skin. The other layer is long and grows over the shorter layer.

Poms come in lots of colors. Orange Poms are a big favorite. Yet Poms come in red, black, chocolate, and other shades as well. Their coats are like rainbows!

This Pom has black, white, and red in its coat.

GIVE YOUR FABULOUS DOG A FITTING NAME

Not sure what to name your Pom? See if any of these names fit your little charmer.

CEDRIC

Mazie   Duchess   Kiki

Bella

Coco   Mischief

BUTCH

GREMLIN   CHIP

Not Just a Pretty Face

Poms are more than pretty. These dogs are also lively and outgoing. They are loyal and smart too. And most Poms are big on boldness. A Pom will bravely defend its owner. It doesn't seem to know it's small.

Poms are cute and tiny, but they have a bold side too.

Poms like to be cuddled. Yet they don't want to sit on someone's lap all day. They are active, curious, and like to explore. Their owners say these dogs have both brains and beauty. They think Poms are the best dogs ever.

CHAPTER TWO

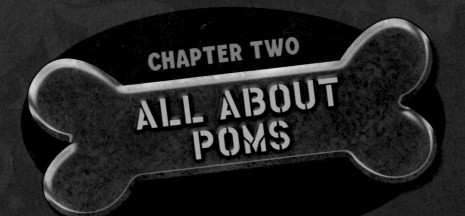

ALL ABOUT POMS

Poms look like little fluff balls. But they didn't start out that way. Poms were once much larger and stronger than they are in modern times.

Early Poms lived in the cold regions near the Arctic. They were hardworking dogs. They pulled sleds and herded reindeer. At night, they acted as watchdogs.

Thomas Gainsborough painted this picture of a Pom and her pup in about 1777.

HELPFUL WOOFERS

Some Poms still work today. They are trained therapy dogs. These pint-sized pooches are taken to hospitals or nursing homes. The patients there cuddle, pet, and play with them. Playing with a pretty Pom can cheer up anyone!

Bigger Isn't Always Better

Over time, people began to breed smaller Poms. Queen Victoria of England loved the little Poms. In the 1880s, she had a few of them.

Queen Victoria holds her Pom, Turi, on her lap during a carriage ride in 1900.

A woman sits near her Pom during a 1913 dog show.

The Perfect Pet and More

Many people wanted little Poms as pets. They were a hit in both Europe and the United States. These dogs won ribbons in dog shows too. They charmed the judges wherever they went.

This perfect Pom won first place in a 1949 dog show.

Toy Dogs

These days, the American Kennel Club (AKC) groups dogs by breed. Dogs that are alike in some ways are grouped together. Some of the AKC's groups are the sporting group, the hound group, and the working group. Poms are in the toy group.

This Afghan hound is in the hound group.

This boxer belongs to the working group.

Springer spaniels, like this one, are in the sporting group.

All the dogs in the toy group are small. Some of them are also quite sturdy and smart. Count the Pom among those.

This woman has a miniature pinscher *(left)* and a Pom *(right)*. Both dogs are in the toy group.

A SUPERSTAR

The year 1988 was great for Poms. A Pom named Great Elms Prince Charming II *(below)* won Best in Show at the Westminster Kennel Club Dog Show. This wonderful winner was four years old and weighed 4.5 pounds (2 kg). He proudly paraded in the show ring and stole the judges' hearts. Prince Charming II was the only Pom ever to win this honor.

BEST IN SHOW
WESTMINSTER KENNEL CLUB FEB 1988

CHAPTER THREE

IS A POMERANIAN YOUR KIND OF DOG?

Poms are pretty pooches. Their owners get lots of attention. Just try walking down the street with one. People will smile and want to pet your dog. They may ask you if your Pom is really a lion that forgot to take its vitamins.

Having a Pom can make you feel special. Yet does that mean you should get one? Before you run out to pick up a Pom, think twice. Decide if a Pom is really your kind of dog.

Little Dogs Don't Mean Little Work

Poms need lots of brushing. Your little powder puff can easily turn into a matted mess. You'll need to brush your Pom every day—even when you're busy or tired.

Regular baths will help keep your Pom's coat clean and fluffy.

Most Pom owners also take their dogs to professional groomers. This can be costly. Be sure your family can afford it.

A groomer brushes a Pom before its appearance in a dog show.

HOUSE DOG

Poms are indoor dogs that need to be around people. They should not be left alone in a yard all day. Poms are happiest with their human family.

Itty-Bitty Noisemakers

Poms are alert dogs that want to protect their owners. This makes them good watchdogs. Some Poms seem to bark at every sound they hear. Many owners don't mind a dog that's a bit noisy. Others can't stand a little "yappy" dog. How do you and your family feel about it?

Poms may not be big, but they can still look fierce! They'll bark and growl if they feel threatened.

Are You Superactive?

Do you love to jog, hike, or bike? Do you dream of doing these things with your dog? If so, don't get a Pom. Poms are active but small. A short walk will do for this short-legged dog. Poms also love to play chase-the-toy.

Not a Sun Lover

Poms are small enough to live in a city apartment.
These dogs can live in the country too. Yet Poms
do not do well in places that are very hot.

Poms get much too warm in hot places.
Their long, thick fur holds in heat.
Too much heat can harm a Pom's
health.

Now you know more about
the Pom. Do you still think
it's the dog for you? If
so, then you're in luck!
A loving and clever
canine is about to
enter your life.

DID YOU KNOW?

Many famous people have thought Poms were the perfect pet. The Italian painter Michelangelo had a Pom. The queen of France, Marie Antoinette, had one too. Well-known composer Wolfgang Amadeus Mozart also owned a Pom. He even wrote music for his beloved dog.

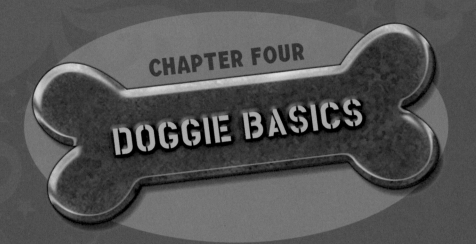

CHAPTER FOUR
DOGGIE BASICS

What day is more fun than both Halloween and the Fourth of July? It's the day you get your Pom!

Make sure to prepare ahead of time. Have supplies on hand to help your new pooch feel at home.

Not sure what you'll need to welcome Fido to your family? This basic list is a great place to start:

- collar

- leash

- tags (for identification)

- dog food

- food and water bowls

- crates (one for when your pet travels by car and one for it to rest in at home)

- treats (to be used in training)

- toys

A Healthy Dog

You'll also want to bring your dog to a veterinarian right away. That's a doctor who treats animals. People call them vets for short.

The vet will give your dog the shots it needs. Bring your Pom back to the vet for checkups or if it becomes ill.

A vet checks out a Pom puppy's ear.

FEEDING TIME TIPS

Ask your vet what to feed your Pom. Dogs need different food at different stages of their lives. And don't feed your dog table scraps. You could end up with a pudgy Pom!

Good food, visits to the vet, and regular exercise will help your Pom stay happy and healthy.

Keeping Your Pom Poofy and Pretty

You may want to find a good groomer for your dog too. Groomers keep Poms' fur looking pretty. They bathe the dogs, brush them, and trim their coats.

Some Pom owners dress their dogs in costumes.

Woofgang Pup aka Bella Luna

TWO FOR YOU?

Some people like to adopt pairs of Poms. Poms get along well with other Poms. The dogs keep each other company when their owners aren't home.

You and Your Pom

Loving your Pom means more than just cuddling that cutie. It also means being a good pet owner. It's fine to spend time with your friends. Just don't forget to feed and walk your Pom first. Your Pom will repay you in many ways. You'll have a loving and loyal friend for years to come.

GLOSSARY

American Kennel Club (AKC): an organization that groups dogs by breed. The AKC also defines the characteristics of different breeds.

breed: a particular type of dog. Dogs of the same breed have the same body shape and general features. *Breed* can also refer to producing puppies.

canine: a dog, or having to do with dogs

coat: a dog's fur

groomer: a person who cleans, brushes, and trims a dog's coat

herd: to make animals move together as a group

matted: severely tangled. If fur is matted, it is clumped together in large masses.

therapy dog: a dog brought to nursing homes or hospitals to comfort patients

toy group: a group of different types of dogs that are all small in size

veterinarian: a doctor who treats animals. Veterinarians are called vets for short.

FOR MORE INFORMATION

Books

Apte, Sunita. *Pomeranian: Pom Pom Ado*. New York: Bearport, 2009. Read all about some remarkable Pomeranians—including Ginger, a 5-pound (2 kg) Pom who fought to defend her owner.

Brecke, Nicole, and Patricia M. Stockland. *Dogs You Can Draw*. Minneapolis: Millbrook Press, 2010. In this title especially for dog lovers, Brecke and Stockland show how to draw many different types of dogs.

Crawley, Dave. *Dog Poems*. Honesdale, PA: Wordsong, 2007. Here's a collection of twenty-four fun poems about dogs.

Gray, Susan H. *Pomeranians*. Mankato, MN: Child's World, 2008. Learn more about Pomeranians in this interesting selection.

Landau, Elaine. *Your Pet Dog*. Rev. ed. New York: Children's Press, 2007. This book is a good guide for young people on choosing and caring for a dog.

Websites

American Kennel Club
http://www.akc.org
Visit this site to find a complete listing of AKC-registered dog breeds, including the Pomeranian. The site also features fun printable activities for kids.

ASPCA Animaland
http://www2.aspca.org/site/PageServer?pagename=kids_pc_home
Check out this page for helpful hints on caring for a dog and other pets.

Index

Photo Acknowledgments

The images in this book are used with the permission of: backgrounds © iStockphoto.com/Julie Fisher and © iStockphoto.com/Tomasz Adamczyk; © iStockphoto.com/Michael Balderas, p. 1; © Jon Fisher/Workbook Stock/Getty Images, pp. 4, 10; © Paul Baldesare/Alamy, p. 5 (top); © Image Register 044/Alamy, p. 5 (bottom); © Aleksey Gorbatenkov/Dreamstime.com, p. 6 (bottom); © Ted Russell/Photographer's Choice/Getty Images, pp. 6-7, 8; © iStockphoto.com/Nancy Mulnix, p. 7; © Tim DeFrisco/Stellar Stock/Photolibrary, p. 9; © Tate, London/Art Resource, NY, p. 11; © TopFoto/The Image Works, p. 12 (top); © Hulton-Deutsch Collection/CORBIS, p. 12 (bottom); Mary Evans Picture Library/Thomas Fall/Everett Collection, p. 13; © Eric Isselée/Dreamstime.com, p. 14 (left); © Jerry Shulman/SuperStock , p. 14 (center); © iStockphoto.com/Eric Isselée, p. 14 (right); © Ron Chapple Studios/Dreamstime.com, p. 15 (top); © Bettmann/CORBIS, p. 15 (bottom); © George Doyle/ Stockbyte/Getty Images, p. 16; © Thomas Del Brase/Photographer's Choice/Getty Images, p. 17; © GK Hart/Vikki Hart/Stone/Getty Images, p. 18 (top); © Nic Neish/Dreamstime.com, p. 18 (bottom); AP Photo/Mary Altaffer, p. 19 (top); © iStockphoto.com/Michelle Milliman, p. 19 (bottom); © Sergey Kolesnikov/Dreamstime.com, p. 20 (top); © Eric Isselée-Fotolia.com, p. 20 (bottom); © Michelle Milliman/Dreamstime.com, p. 21; © orchidpoet/Alamy, p. 22; © Sam Panthaky/AFP/Getty Images, p. 23 (top); © Yoshio Tomii/SuperStock, p. 23 (bottom); © Inti St. Clair/Photodisc/Getty Images, p. 24; © Tooties/Dreamstime.com, p. 25 (top); © Uturnpix/Dreamstime.com, p. 25 (2nd from top); © iStockphoto.com/orix3, p. 25 (2nd from bottom); © Katrina Brown/Dreamstime.com, p. 25 (bottom); © Flirt/SuperStock, p. 26; © Ling Xia/Dreamstime.com, p. 27 (main); © Jay Zee/Shutterstock Images, p. 27 (inset); © Robyn Beck/AFP/Getty Images, p. 28 (top); © Michelle D. Milliman/Shutterstock Images, p. 28 (bottom).

Front cover: © Jon Fisher/Workbook Stock/Getty Images.
Back cover: © American Images Inc./Digital Vision/Getty Images.